PEOPLE

**For a free color catalog describing Gareth Stevens'
list of high-quality books and multimedia programs,
call 1-800-542-2595 (USA) or 1-800-461-9120 (Canada).
Gareth Stevens Publishing's Fax: (414) 225-0377.
See our catalog, too, on the World Wide Web:
http://gsinc.com**

Library of Congress Cataloging-in-Publication Data

Stickland, Paul.
    People / Paul Stickland.
       p. cm. — (Working)
    Includes index.
    Summary: Describes the work of people in various
occupations.
       ISBN 0-8368-2157-2 (lib. bdg.)
       1. Occupations—Juvenile literature. 2. Professions—Juvenile
literature. [1. Occupations.] I. Title. II. Series: Stickland, Paul.
Working.
    HF5381.2.S84   1998
    331.7'02—dc21   98-13656

This North American edition first published in 1998 by
Gareth Stevens Publishing
1555 North RiverCenter Drive, Suite 201
Milwaukee, Wisconsin 53212 USA

© 1991 by Paul Stickland. Designed by Herman Lelie.
Produced by Mathew Price Ltd.,
The Old Glove Factory, Bristol Road,
Sherborne, Dorset DT9 4HP, England.
Additional end matter © 1998 by Gareth Stevens, Inc.

Gareth Stevens series editor: Dorothy L. Gibbs
Editorial assistant: Diane Laska

Printed in Hong Kong

1 2 3 4 5 6 7 8 9 02 01 00 99 98

WORKING

PEOPLE

Paul Stickland

Gareth Stevens Publishing
MILWAUKEE

J 331.7
ST

Office workers use telephones and
computers to help them run businesses.

Fishermen use nets to catch fish from the depths of the ocean.

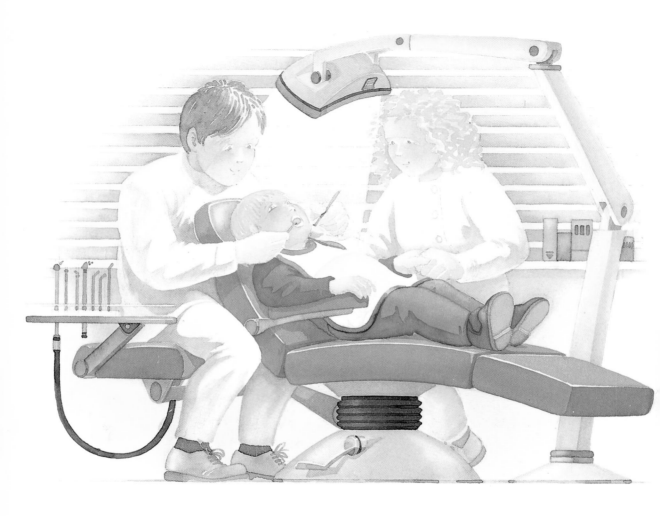

Dentists clean and repair our teeth with special tools to keep them healthy.

A dump truck driver can empty a load
of gravel right where you want it.

Gardeners plant seeds in their gardens
to grow flowers, fruits, and vegetables.

8

With a lot of care, the flowers bloom,
and the fruits and vegetables ripen.

A hairdresser can style hair short, long,
smooth, curly — many different ways.

10

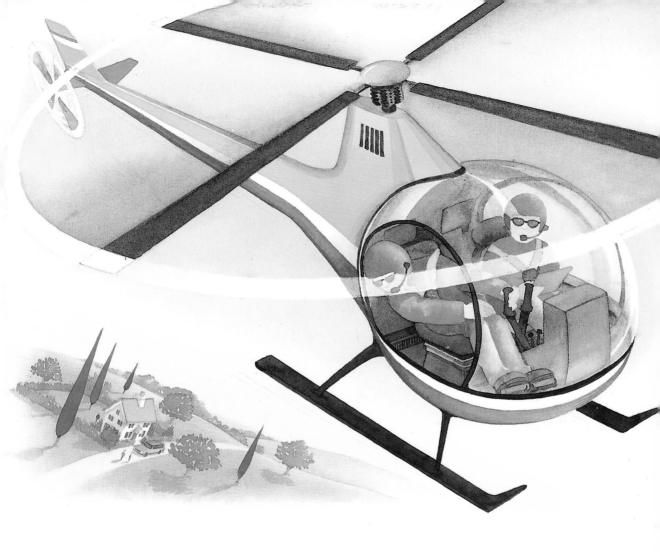

Helicopter pilots can hover in the air to see what is happening on the ground.

Welders use a very hot flame to join pieces of metal together. Special clothes protect them from sparks.

Bakers make delicious breads and cakes.
They bake them in hot ovens.

Divers explore the ocean. They carry air to breathe in a tank on their back.

They wear goggles to protect their eyes,
and rubber suits to keep them warm.

GLOSSARY

depths — places that are in the deepest part of something.

goggles — special glasses that fit tightly against the face around the eyes to keep out things like wind, dirt, and water.

hover — to stay in one place up in the air, hanging over a certain place on the ground below.

pilot — a person who flies an airplane, a helicopter, or some other kind of aircraft.

protect — to keep away from danger or harm.

ripen — to grow until ready for picking or using.

style (v) — to fix or arrange in a certain way or design.

INDEX